ONCE IN A
WIFETIME

STEPHANIE ANNE MELLO

PublishAmerica
Baltimore

First printing

ISBN: 1-60441-998-9 (copyright)
ISBN: 978-1-61582-075-7 (hardcover)
PUBLISHED BY PUBLISHAMERICA, LLLP
www.publishamerica.com
Baltimore

Printed in the United States of America

DEDICATION

There is so much attention given to the military effort whenever the Armed Forces are engaged in a military conflict, but during the routine living of military spouses and families, their stories often go untold. "Warrior" is a term often applied to the actual soldiers, Marines, seamen and sailors who do battle. This book is dedicated to those warriors who do battle on another front, the home front. More specifically it is a tribute to the husbands and wives, lovers, parents and children of soldiers, those courageous men and women who serve in the United States Army, Army Reserve and National Guard.

These dedicated "warriors" engage the enemy of loneliness, fear, despair and isolation constantly. They are the men and women who struggle daily to maintain home and hearth, whether it is in their day-to-day living or during a publicized battle. It is not always easy as the greatest constant in their lives is change. They fight the battles of anxiety, survival and separation every day. Armed only with personal commitment, intestinal fortitude and conviction, they triumph over the negative military images, anti-warrior sentiments and apathetic social attitudes with dignity, grace and decorum.

There are no medals for these unsung heroes (cliché maybe—but true). Their success (and failure) is measured on an unseen chart—the chart of the heart. It is to those who have loved, lost and survived throughout their own personal battles that this book is dedicated. Enclosed in these pages are stories gathered through the years of the hope, joys, sadness and frustrations that many military spouses face on a daily basis. The changes and adjustments that must be made, the struggles to maintain a stable family and marriage, the successes and the not so successful attempts to adapt to a lifestyle unlike any other encountered.

It is to these heroes, and especially the ladies of the 3d Brigade, 3d Infantry Division, and 1st Battalion, 30th and 15 Infantry Regiments, that I owe my survival as a military spouse. And to one very special former military spouse—who gave me the tools I needed to wage my own battles and emerge victorious, who constantly encouraged me to continue in my efforts to publish these stories—Jane, my mother. Thanks, Mom—for supporting me, my family and our way of life and for helping me to make the right choices.

And last, but certainly not least, I dedicate this to my children, and the thousands of other military children, whom I have learned through time suffer the same hardships, endure the same challenges and overcome the obstacles that we face every day, without notoriety, sometimes without even simple praise and recognition. You are a rare breed and I am so very proud of you all.

INTRODUCTION

I recently attended a retirement ceremony for a Soldier and friend, who, after 30 years in the military, was leaving the Army for new challenges in the civilian world. Accompanied by his wife, a woman of average height, weight and appearance, he stood proud and tall, his uniform starched so stiff it could have stood by itself, as the retirement order was read. Speakers noted his distinguished career, his many assignments and accomplishments, the people whose lives he had touched and the experiences they had personally and professionally shared with him. I listened intently as he thanked all the people in his life, including his commander, the NCOs who trained him, the soldiers who served under him, and even his minister, who had made it possible for him to achieve this goal.

As he finished his laundry list of thank-you's I had to admit I was impressed all the way to my socks, but one question gnawed at me—where was his wife during all of this time? Not once during the ceremony, nor in the long list of thanks and acknowledgments, did the Soldier take the moment to congratulate or thank her for the part she played in his life. Many would say that it was not her "moment," that she had not earned the honor and should be glad to stand in the shadows on such a momentous occasion.

Historically that is where many military wives spend their days—in the shadows of their soldiers, airmen, sailors or Marines. It is a time-honored tradition to recognize the sacrifice, dedication, and devotion of the service member, but not the wife. I often have images of a serviceman who bore, raised and reared his children without a wife. This brave warrior coordinated all the movers, packers, rental agreements, transportation appointments, dental and doctor visits, veterinarian visits, school activities and home life. I believe he also administered all discipline, home health remedies, and healing of the hearts for first love and lost loves. This seasoned combat veteran also explained to small children why the other parent could not make it to their school play/parent lunch/field trip/choir recital/open house/graduation or other important life action. Is it any wonder he was receiving such honors now? With his commitment to God and country it must have been almost impossible for him to do it all alone.

Fortunately for most men, there has emerged the one human being who could, and often did, do all these things without benefit of a full-time partner in the house and usually with even less recognition—the military wife. Originally many people did not even know they existed—unless they were closely involved in that circle of silent supporters. Success of their military mates was their reward—at the time. However, times are changing and many wives are now beginning to stand and demand acknowledgment for their contribution to the continued success of their service member and the military. No longer satisfied to stand ten paces behind, silent and subjective, these women are becoming more visible and viable as a source of manpower, information, support and success for the military. It has been a long time coming and in many respects has been evolving since the days of Bess Truman and Mamie Eisenhower.

WHAT IS THE
MILITARY WIFE?

As the wife of a career Soldier with more than twenty-six years in service, the daughter of a retired Air Force Sergeant, and a veteran of the Navy and Army in my own right, I have seen, heard and been a party to many adjustments, changes and crises in the military community. We have survived twenty-eight deployments, including four in hazardous countries. We have moved eleven times in twenty years and have met hundreds of wonderful, strong, intelligent and thriving women and men who have enhanced, strengthened and improved our lives more than a hundred fold.

There are those who would say that being a military wife is no more difficult than being the wife of a civilian—that it is much the same as being the wife of a truck driver, doctor, lawyer or construction worker. While no one in "our world" believes that any marriage is a cake walk, it takes a very special person to be able to survive the life a military wife accepts when she takes her vows and signs "on the dotted line." There are hardships, separations, fears, multiple moves, sole parenting days, adjustments to foreign lands and languages and learning new tax and driving laws every three years.

Like most husbands and wives we get angry, frustrated, agitated, hormonal, torqued and re-torqued. We cry, laugh, hug, fear, and love just like other women—we just do it at a different pace and place than most. We pack up our lives in 3x5 cardboard boxes, hoping that the "Little Mermaid" statue we bought in Denmark makes it intact to our new destination. We pray that the clay molds of our children's hands survive just one more move. We do battle with our consciences and weight limits as we try to determine which memories are more valuable than others and which can be sacrificed. We bid tearful good-byes to friends and neighbors knowing that we may never meet or hear from some of them ever again.

Our children stomp and cry as they are torn from the life they have just begun to get comfortable with—again. Family pets are taken to new homes as oftentimes they are not allowed where we are going.

We find ourselves thrust into new cities, states, and countries with little preparation or warning and are told how fortunate we are to travel to such foreign and exotic locations. We learn new school and teacher names, navigate new city streets, adopt new communities and make new friends while promising to keep in touch with the old. Once again we try to locate the best and least expensive places to shop. Adapt, adjust, and overcome become the theme words and focus of their lives...and for the most part we do it well.

This is a tribute to the women, and in more recent times, the men, who have taken the backseat to service, to Corps and to country. They have done it voluntarily, many with little foreknowledge of the obstacles ahead. It is a compilation of their lives and what they encountered. It will make you laugh, sometimes make you cry, and hopefully make you understand the strength, courage and moral fiber that comes together and is the human being proud to be called a military wife.

INITIAL ENTRY

All the posters, videos and hype cannot prepare anyone for life as a military spouse. Even being a military "brat" cannot teach you everything you need to know. Once a civilian takes the final oath and "ships out" to basic training, life as it was before is no more. Suddenly there are new phrases, terms and words, acronyms that must be learned and dedicated to memory. Moving becomes a constant part of your world.

From day one military spouses learn how to survive on their own. Friends and family cannot begin to fathom the inevitable changes that are happening in your life. While the new recruit is off at basic training learning how to be a Soldier, a warrior, the family remains behind. Trash still goes out, parent-teacher meetings still go on, lives continue, but what was done as a team is now done alone. During the first weeks of training there is minimal, if any, contact outside of letters quickly written or a short, cryptic phone call. While the Soldier focuses on training and mission, the family continues to focus on making it through every day with little or no contact or support.

Once basic training is completed, the Soldier then moves on to advanced individual training (AIT)—yet more time away from family. Contact with the Soldier is more readily available, phones calls are made freely (on off-duty time), and weekends and holidays can be spent together—if geography allows. The time away can be as little as six weeks and as much as one year, dependent upon the specialization the Soldier has chosen. It is a phenomenally stressful time, but necessary. What carries most spouses through is the knowledge that at the end of all the training the Soldier and family will be reunited and move forward in their chosen new lives. It definitely gives new meaning to that part of the wedding vow that states "through good times and bad."

WEDDING VOWS

Go to any wedding, whether in a chapel, court house or church and you will most likely hear blushing brides, bedecked in white, uttering the same words that so many have said before them. Love, honor, cherish, through sickness and in health, blah, blah, blah. Pretty much the standard-issue promise that lovers make when they are—well—in love and the world is filled with nothing but thoughts of their beloved.

Military wives are not really any different in that regard—but the promises that they make should be a little more realistic—just to prepare them. Reading the "real deal" version of the military wedding would at least provide some insight into what is yet to come. Vows written and exchanged according to the reality of the world they are about to enter might read something like this:

"I, (state your name), take you, (state his name), as my lawful wedded husband, (upon approval of your company commander and once validated by entry in the Defense Enrollment Eligibility Reporting System (DEERS)). I promise to love, honor, and cherish you through richer or poorer, sickness and in health, (I will understand that this is not your fault, but usually preceded by non-receipt of pay for a variety of reasons to include collection of overpayment of travel allowances, overpayment or nonpayment of Basic Allowances for Housing, glitches in the computer or improper filing on the part of someone else), till deployment, temporary duty (TDY), field problem, military school, unit lock-downs, early morning PT rises, late-night training meetings or inventory/ maintenance sections us do part. I love you enough to voluntarily surrender my personal identify in lieu of yours. I shall surrender my social security card, along with my maiden name, upon issue of my DD 1172—Military Identification Card application form. I will remove all other traces of my previous existence and individuality and draw it out only upon your release, discharge or retirement from the military. I will faithfully teach your social security number to our children, should time and mission requirements permit us having children, so that they may recite it upon command. I will carry and defend my military dependent identification card, protecting it from all others, while producing it on demand at a variety of military shopping centers, command checkpoints and access ways. I will learn not to cringe, flinch or cry out loud in public every time someone refers to me or our children as 'dependents.' I will learn to fit our 10,000 pounds of household furnishings into 1,100 square feet of space. I will adapt, adjust and overcome moves to countries whose language I cannot speak, endure lack of physical intimacy because you have worked a thirty-six-hour shift and are too tired to open your eyes let alone put a sparkle in mine. I will tolerate and abide, with minimal complaint, a variety of short-notice 'missions' without knowing where you are going or when you are coming back, moving from state to state every time the military deems fit to assign you someplace new. I vow to learn 150 or more abbreviations for military words and phrases and to know what those terms and phrases mean. I will graciously and supportively accompany you to a slew of military briefings, meetings, functions, balls, hails and farewells, where soldiers will be recognized and honored while wives sit in the shadows, wearing patented smiles and clapping at the appropriate moments, eye candy for the masses. I will walk your dog; wash your car; launder your socks, uniforms, and other military gear, insuring that it is cleaned, ironed and/or starched to a military standard. I will raise our children, with your occasional intervention at important family gatherings. I will weather, with a smile, missed Christmases, birthdays, anniversaries, Mother's Days, Halloween parties, Easter celebrations, family dinners, graduations, reunions, weddings, births, funerals, and a wide assortment of other social gatherings that rank lower on the profile for attendance. I will stop whether in my car or on foot whenever 'colors' are played, stand tall and proud, with hand over heart, and pay tribute to each and every flag that passes by. I will understand that you are not prone to outward displays of emotions or affections unless a sporting event or several profane terms are involved. I also know in my heart that the love that drew us together will carry us through the times that are to come. I will remember that there is no one in the world I would rather spend my days with than you whether it be in blue jeans or BDUs and that I will hold closely that time spent, as tomorrow could be our last. I will vigilantly maintain a constantly changing address book (or roster as you prefer to call it) with the names of people we will always remember and even some that I would rather forget. I will devoutly, publicly and personally support and defend your right to choose this lifestyle to my friends, families, co-workers, strangers on the street, radicals in the market square, little old ladies in the supermarket, anti-military organizations and our children, as the patriotic path you have chosen to take. In the end I will stand quietly in the rear as your accomplishments are paraded before the masses and mine remain obscure. I will walk the military life trail with you and help you to cross back over into the civilian world when your time is done. This is your life and the life I have chosen to support until the end of my days or the expiration date of my ID card as set forth by military policy."

THE FIRST DUTY STATION

For many new military husbands and wives the move to the first duty station is a solitary one. Most are younger men and women, coming straight out of their childhood homes into a new, exciting and unimaginable adventure.

Arrival at a first duty station is an eye-opening and life-changing experience. The Soldier is whisked through a short in-processing, assigned to a unit, introduced to his or her supervisors (chain of command) and the wheels turn to integrate the new arrival into the workings of the unit. He or she is issued the equipment needed to insure job performance, escorted to all the places necessary to ensure success of his mission and is swiftly made another working component of the unit.

Meanwhile, back at the ranch, or hotel or guest house, the newly displaced spouse sits alone, reading through phone books, pamphlets, and relocation packets. He or she may be adventurous enough to leave her cloistered space and journey to the local food court or shoppette. Uniformed soldiers move about swiftly as new surroundings are purveyed, trying to read the map provided in the welcome packet. Cars with license plates from all across the nation fill the parking lot and he or she begins to wonder if anyone is actually from the state they will call home for the next three years. As quickly as exploration of the "new world," the spouse retreats once more to the safety of temporary lodgings to wait for the Soldier to return. In the darkness the spouse rocks slowly in the lounge chair, unseen tears flow freely, as she/he weeps and wonders if life will ever be "normal" again.

WHY WE CHOOSE THE MILITARY LIFE

With all the aggravation, frustration and confusion that is encountered when someone marries "into the military," the question often arises as to why. Why marry someone who is going to be gone all the time? Why travel from city to city, country to country, at a moment's notice? Why abandon your family, friends and roots to go with a *stranger* to a different way of life, a different way of living? Why put yourself into a position where you *know* that you, your children, your home and even the dog are going to be a secondary priority? Many say it's because we have sins we need to be punished for—but I argue against that philosophy.

For many spouses the answer is simple—this is the person we have chosen to spend our lives with and this is their profession—so we make the choice. We choose the way of life, we choose it for ourselves and for our children. We choose to defend it, to protect and preserve it. We choose to preserve the past, and our family histories, but walk away from it while looking toward the future and building a better and stronger future.

Will it prepare us for the adventure we are about to embark on? Probably not. Will it always seem worth the effort, the tears, the fears and compromises that we confront on a daily basis—absolutely not. Will there be days when we will stare at the heavens, posing the question to the powers that be: "What did I ever do to you?" Of course there will be. Will there be days when sanity checks will cause us to reconsider our choices and wonder what in the name of the heavens were we thinking when we took on this challenge? Sure, you'd have to be a zombie not to have these thoughts. What functioning, thinking, feeling human being would not challenge their choice to live this lifestyle multiple times a year, often in a day? And then the day ends, colors are played, final formations are over and the Soldier walks back through the front door, "draggin' butt, dog tired," parks his duffel bag by the back door and crashes on the couch and we remember why we made the choice.

A HISTORY OF SERVICE

For some of us marrying into the military is not a choice—it's in our genetic makeup. My father made his first career in the Air Force, all my uncles served in some military for at least six years, and both my brothers served in the Army.

I was in the Navy during the tail end of Viet Nam and moved to the Army several years later. It was there that I met my husband. I was born in a military hospital, as were my sister and brothers, my sons and daughter. My son serves in the Army and his twin brother served in the Air Force. All my grandchildren were born in military medical facilities. It would not surprise me to learn that our blood is camouflage, not red and that our life was pre-determined the day we were born. Many of the men and women I have met through the years echo the same sentiment. Sons, daughters, mothers and fathers are born into the life of the military family. It was not just an occupational choice, but a way of life bred into us for generations. There were times when we all tried to walk away from this chaotic and often stressful lifestyle, but somehow it always called us back to it. I guess there were just too many military chromosomes in our gene pool to make it any other way.

WHAT MAKES US
DIFFERENT

The Army spouse (and family) differs from the civilian one, and even those families in other military services, in many ways. How we respond to crises, how we maneuver and manipulate our calendars to support not just school activities and family life, but also deployments, field exercises and special military family events is probably more intense than our civilian counterparts. Additionally, much of what we do—we do alone.

The military spouse can pack fifteen years of living, 12,000 pounds of personal property and two dogs in three days, while clearing children out of local schools, clearing base agencies and writing out change of address cards (normally without the assistance of the previously mentioned military sponsor).

Upon arrival at a new home, the military spouse

can unpack the same fifteen years of living, 12,000 pounds of property and have children re-enrolled in school—all within three days. Generally speaking we do not feel settled until photos of Junior, Mom, Dad and the dog are displayed properly on the appropriate counter and our walls are decorated with images of our Soldier.

The military spouse goes to sleep at night, often alone, and prays for her soldier's safe return. Phone calls and knocks at the door are often met with apprehension, especially during a deployment, when either could mean that the spouse's life has changed forever due to the death of a Soldier.

Friends we have made are held close to our hearts and address books are covered in white-out or written in pencil as they change so frequently.

The Army spouse goes to their high school reunion, speaking a language totally foreign to their former classmates who remained in the same town for twenty-plus years and realizes that no one ever really goes "home again."

Letters, notes, and cards from the Soldier are opened slowly, held closely and stored in our hearts and memory boxes—which continue to grow in number with each deployment.

Words, and their impact, take on closer and new

meaning—global terrorism, casualty, loss, incident, separation, deployment, unity, honor, loyalty. They have more intense meanings to us.

The military wife can tell you the difference between a bullet-proof vest and Kevlar and can tell you which is better and where to buy it.

He/she can pack fifteen pounds of love into a shoebox to be mailed to a single Soldier in the unit so he/she doesn't feel forgotten.

Watching the news is not an option for the military spouse—it's a daily obligation and curse rolled up into one—wanting to stay abreast of the news and praying—because no news really is good news.

Our families routinely learn time differences between the United States and foreign countries to make sure we and they are not calling in the dark hours of the night when making a telephone call. Our cars bear support stickers 365 days a year and yellow ribbons wrap around our hearts not just our trees. We cannot hear taps without our eyes misting. We know the history and meaning of the colors of the flag, and our children include military units in their family lineage. We wave those flags, not just when it is popular or in support of a cause, but because it symbolizes our way of life.

We struggle with many of the same challenges as our civilian counterparts and those in other services. We face many of the same obstacles and fears—money to pay the bills, how to put three children through college on one salary because once again we have given up a good paying job to be with our Soldier, living far away from an ailing or aging parent or sibling, how much longer will the tires last on our seven-year-old car and what will we do if something happens to our spouse? The major difference is once again—we usually do it alone.

MILITARY SPOUSE VERSUS MARRIED TO THE MILITARY

Even within our own ranks there are differences, there are military spouses and those who are "married to the military." Military life is not for everyone, it takes a very special breed of human being to endure all the changes and challenges that occur on a daily basis. I used to believe that I knew all that, but life as a military spouse and as a mom of a Soldier changed my opinion.

Very early in his Soldier life, my son took a wife, a young, immature, precarious girl, with attitudes and opinions of her own. I remember standing on the front lawn of our government quarters, arguing, rather loudly, that the young woman before me was not the "military spouse" he needed, that she, Erika, did not possess the "right stuff" that he would need to support him. As with so many other challenges in life, I was wrong. I have watched over the past twelve years as this child evolved into a phenomenal force of nature, a consummate volunteer, and total military spouse. She has endured his and her injuries, their constant moves and the changes. She has sent him off to battle, waged her own battle of loneliness, raised two wonderful children (who now call me Grandma). She truly embodies the military spouse persona.

Others, who are "married to the military" are not so fortunate. They see the glamour of travel, the draw of the uniform and believe that they have what it takes to be a military spouse, only to learn too late that it is not all parades, adventure and excitement. They are the "casualties of war," personal, professional and career wars. The long hours, constant duty away from home, separation from family, and long nights alone, win the battle against commitment and care. No blame, no fault, just the way it happens. As I said earlier, it takes a very special, strong and enduring personality to become a military spouse, male or female regardless. It takes strength, endurance, loyalty and love to survive.

HOW CAN THE
TWO COMPARE?

With the world situation constantly changing, the separation of Soldier and family continues to weigh heavily upon the marriage bonds of the military family. One young woman, married to a truck driver, told me that she understood how hard it was to live alone so much. Another, the wife of a marketing executive, shared with me that her husband was gone just as much as mine. Yet another woman, married to a computer technician, informed me that her husband was away from home just as often as my Soldier, but her husband didn't get all the extra pay that soldiers get for deploying to foreign countries. She said she didn't understand why soldiers got all that extra money, just for doing their jobs. I thanked her for opinion and fought back the tears and the urge to shout, "Lady—you don't have a clue! The next time your husband goes to work and his computer fires a weapon at him, let me know. As you kiss your spouse good-bye each morning, which I haven't done for six months, do you worry that he will kick in the door of an insurgent wanting nothing more than to sacrifice himself and my Soldier for the glory of his faith? My Soldier faces people daily who smile at him on the streets just before they start shooting at him, working around things that blow up without warning, and often the very people he is putting his life on the line for berate and belittle him." Instead, I just smiled, insincerely, and walked away.

WHAT WE MISS
THE MOST

Friends and family, who gather weekly to share dinner, go to church or just sit on the front porch talking.

Neighborhood barbeques with old classmates, trading stories on how our children have changed since we were in school.

Weddings, births, and anniversaries come and go frequently without our soldier's presence. The growing up of nieces and nephews, the aging of our parents and the growing of their grandchildren— the passage of time is swift and seems even swifter with each subsequent move that takes us further away from our childhood homes.

Family reunions often go off without us as we are usually too far away, or our military paycheck won't support the expense of flying or driving all of us to join in the celebrations.

The only roots we have are in our hearts—our lives, and our roots are portable. Knowing the mailman, butcher and parish minister, having lifelong friends who went to the same schools, attended the same parties, worked in the same company are luxuries afforded only to those who do not live the "portable life."

These are but a few of the things we miss as we travel from city to city, country to country, in support of our husbands and their duty.

WITHER THOU GO, SO SHALL I

Sarah has lived in once city the entire twenty-six years of her life. She recently married a Soldier, is expecting their first child, her parents' first grandchild, and knows that within weeks of the baby's birth that she and her husband will be moving across the country for stationing. "I don't know if I'm ready or able to do this—leave my family—especially now with the baby coming. But this is where my hubby goes, so I will go too."

Tiffany sits in her two-bedroom quarters; her infant son, Grant, sleeps quietly in his crib while his big brother, Mason, watches yet another episode of *Barney.* Her husband, Steve, is on rotation in the desert—again—for two weeks. His job as an Observer/Controller at Fort Irwin, California, requires that he be gone two weeks of every month. Living in the middle of the desert affords little entertainment opportunity and the nearest town is thirty-seven miles away. "Knowing that this is a short-term assignment makes the isolation a little easier to deal with, but not much. Sometimes you just want to pack up everything, jump in the car and run home—and then you remember—you already are home."

Andrew waits, sometimes patiently, sometimes not, to receive word from his Soldier that housing is available in the little Italian town outside his wife's new duty station. Because of the shortage of homes in the area and the high cost of living on the Italian economy, Andrew and his daughter, Lily, must wait until government housing is open to them. "I'm excited about seeing another part of the world, but hate being apart from my wife. We (spouses) don't always get to move with our Soldier—and that's one of the hardest parts—waiting again for the Army to decide how our lives will change."

Stephanie walks the streets of the little German town she now calls home. Stumbling through the language, she explores the Metzgerei (butcher shop), bakerei (bakery) and kleidung geshaft (clothing stores), endures the glares of those who don't understand her broken German and returning the smiles of those who understand why soldiers still remain in Europe. She walks the two miles back to her economy housing, places her purchases in cabinets and "shrunks" (German homes don't have closets) and walks to the local strawberry field with her children to pick the fresh fruit and enjoy the waning sunshine. Her former home in Brooklyn, New York, with mom-and-pop shops, pizza parlors and major department stores, seems a lifetime away. As she washes the dirt and dust away from the fresh-picked fruit, her children watch the local cartoon channel, visiting with her new friend and neighbor, Petra's son and daughter. Petra's English is broken and often hard to understand but the adult contact helps Stephanie to further adjust to living in a foreign country. Petra's children don't speak English, Stephanie's children don't speak German, but it doesn't seem to matter to any of them as they enjoy the cartoon show.

Whether to Colorado, Texas, Italy or Germany, we go wherever the Army sends our Soldier. We adapt to the local community as much as possible, accept it as our own and become part of it. Volunteering or working for pay, minimal or maximum involvement, we are learning and living new lives all the time. Some places we drive away from, vowing never to return while others take hold of our hearts and become a permanent part of our "I'd love to return here" lists. Wherever we come from, wherever we go to, we carry with us parts of the people, the places and the memories with us. It helps us to remember why we do what we do—and helps us to get through it all.

FEAR FOR OUR OWN

My feet had barely crossed the threshold of my apartment building when my neighbor, Elsa, came running up the stairs of our German housing complex. My heart skipped a beat as she fumbled in broken German and English words, "Shtepanie—did you hear about the Mello Man," her affectionate term for my husband. Since our husbands were both assigned to the same combat zone in Kuwait, I immediately feared that he had been injured or worse. "Noooo," escaped almost as whisper from my throat as I grabbed the stairwell rail to regain my balance. Her words, and the emotions etched in her face, told me that something serious had happened and Mark was involved. What had he done, or worse yet, what had been done to him? "I jest get off da phone mit my husband and he tell me dey gonna give da Mello Man the Silber Schtar!" Okay—so was this a posthumous award? I knew they didn't give these medals to guys just hanging around on the battlefield and visions of Mark, injured or worse, suddenly flooded my mind. Images of the last time I saw him, the first time I saw him raced through my brain. Would I see him again? The many late-night pre-deployment conversations we had had, mulling over the potential for harm, the fears I had, the fears he had. The driving need he had to go and do what he had trained to do for more than twelve years was suddenly as vivid as if we had talked about it yesterday. I remembered telling him the day he left that the Army had given him a huge vehicle, covered in armor plating, for a reason—to stay in it and stay safe. Words to the folk song "Billy, Don't Be a Hero," suddenly popped into my head.

The next few minutes of what Elsa said did not reach me until she said, "He's okay." My face must have gone totally pale as Elsa then asked me, "You okay?" I don't remember holding my breath but immediately released what felt like the air at the bottom of a ball when the plug is let out, a gust almost, reminding me to breathe and inhale again. I also realized that I had a death-hold on my lower lip with my teeth when the pain of that grip shot through the bottom of my mouth.

It wasn't until several weeks later that I received a letter from Mark that said, "I am sure that by now you have heard many stories of what happened and how I was awarded the Bronze Star with Valor. Please ignore what has probably been blown way out of proportion. I was just doing my job." It was at that moment that I truly realized that I was married to a Soldier, a real Soldier, who believed that his job was defending his country, no matter the risk.

LEARNING HOW TO "TALK THE TALK"

Every culture has its own slang and jargon and the military is no different. Acronyms seem to replace the common words and even some of the uncommon ones for just about everything. Learning to understand this talk is the job of a lifetime.

THE BRIEFING

The Company Commander stood before the audience of young women, children and soldiers gathered in the theater for a deployment briefing. He was finishing up his briefing of the families on an upcoming deployment that the soldiers had been tasked to do. Charlene, a petite and usually calm and sedate young woman, sat in the auditorium/ battalion conference room, listening intently to everything he had to say, taking notes in her brown leather day planner as he spoke, highlighting events and times that he stressed as important. When the commander decided he had dispensed as much information concerning the TOC, POC, FRG, RD, LES, POA, ACS, and other general family concerns, he made the gravest of all errors—he asked for questions. Charlene timidly pushed her hand into the air and was immediately called upon. "I hate to ask this, sir—but could you explain to me what you just said—in English this time?"

ON THE MOVE AGAIN

"Home" is a short-term phrase for military families, especially in the Army. Routinely military families can expect to move every three years at a minimum. This creates a mindset that requires us to establish short and portable family roots, invest in rewriteable or removeable address pages in our phone books and explains why we refer to our days as "at this duty station."

Boxes and crates are packed to the breaking points of wooden crates. Memories of a lifetime are wrapped and taped in cartons. When a military family moves, it is not just "stuff" that goes into the moving van, but our lives and the substance of those lives.

When the movers arrived at our home for the third move of our military careers I thought that I had the system down pat. Glassware and breakables on one side of the house, high cost valuables listed separately, "Do Not Pack" items closed up in a closet with a big sign that said "Do Not Open" on the door. I had learned early in the moving process to insure that my packers were well fed and usually gave away the wines and spirits that could not be packed or shipped. Somehow this seemed to inspire the people handling my precious treasures to do so with a much gentler hand.

On this particular occasion, as we prepared to move from Alabama to Germany, my first overseas journey as a military wife, I made sure to have everything carefully placed and marked. I watched like a veritable hawk as every item was wrapped, numbered and placed in its box. I signed the seals as the boxes marked kitchen, dining room, bedroom and bath, were placed and secured into the wooden crates that would be their temporary home until they were safe within my new dwelling, more than 3,000 miles away. Safe in the knowledge that I had been fully prepared, I signed the inventory forms as the movers closed up the van and drove off with the treasures of my life in their hands.

Once we arrived in Germany and housing arrangements had been made, I anxiously awaited the delivery date of my household goods. It had been six weeks since I had laid eyes upon the plaster cast of my three-year-old daughter's hand and the photographs of my great-grandparents in Ireland. When the vans finally arrived in front of my home and began unloading my things I understood how Maureen O'Hara's character in *The Quiet Man* felt as my things were unwrapped and inspected for nicks and scratches. Suddenly I detected a faint odor—like bad fruit—coming from one particular crate.

With each new box the odor became stronger and more pungent. After four boxes were removed from the crate it became almost unbearable until the fifth box was removed and opened. In their zeal to pack everything, the movers had packed my trashcan— before I got a chance to empty it!

EVEN OUR CHILDREN ADJUST

Our 1991 move from Germany to California was one mixed with emotions and chaos. Having just returned from the Gulf War, my husband was advised that the Kaserne, where we had spent the last three and a half years would be returned to the German government and we had to move out fast!

With less than thirty days to depart country, we made transportation appointments, cleaned our quarters, vaccinated pets, cleaned cars from front axle to exhaust pipe and sorted through household goods once again for "keepers and tossers." Our daughter, Brianna, age six, was moping about because once again her birthday party had been shifted to accommodate yet another move. As the movers strategically packed and pulled boxes, Bri was constantly shushed aside and asked to move.

As the apartment emptied of our possessions, we

realized that we had not heard Bri whine or shuffle about for a while. Searching the house, we came up empty. We checked the park, the hall and the basement, but found no sign of Bri. Panicking and ready to call the Polizei (German Police), my husband grabbed my arm, raised his finger to his lips, and gently maneuvered me to the balcony where we had placed the "Do Not Pack" items from our home. Nestled there, in the extra large air kennel we bought to ship our dog, sleeping soundly with "Mr. Binky" and a pillow, was our daughter. It proved once again how adaptable the military child becomes.

GOING, GOING, GONE— FIELD EXERCISES AND DEPLOYMENTS

Operations Enduring Freedom, Anaconda, Bright Star, Ahaus Tara I, II and III, Provide Comfort, REFORGER, and a host of other titles blare across the headlines of the *Army Times, Stars and Stripes*, local, and national newspapers. The average person glances at the articles and then moves on to the sports or business pages.

For the military wife, however, these titles take on a more personal meaning. It is where their husband is spending or has spent the last three, six or more months. Articles in the papers, news blurbs on television and radio announcements are often the only indicator the military wife has of how her spouse is doing in lands she can't even begin to imagine, probably can't spell and will most likely never add to her vacation list.

With the increase in the military function and mission in today's world it is inevitable that a Soldier will leave home for some length of time, to some unknown point and face any amount of danger.

When soldiers of the Vanguard Battalion, 2d Brigade, 3d Armor Division, Gelnhausen, Germany, deployed to the deserts of Saudi Arabia their wives had been given best and worst case scenarios. Best case—they would go, end the invasion of Kuwait and return home. Worst case—many of them wouldn't come home. The small chapel on Coleman Kaserne filled to near capacity each Sunday, prayers went up and out to soldiers and their families for strength, courage and safety.

Fortunately most of the soldiers returned to their wives and children. Unfortunately, a few did not. When word came down from the command group that a Soldier had been lost in the conflict many wives and soldiers did not know what to say or do. Some distanced themselves in fear that the simple association of death would bring the reality closer to home, while others engaged the chain of concern and began the process of helping a sister in need.

A select few women knew exactly what to do. Rallying around each other, they put aside their own fears and concerns and drew strength from each other to help the soldier's family—a young wife, pregnant with her first child—to weather the loss of her husband.

Meals were prepared, funeral arrangements were made, transportation appointments cleared and legal matters taken into hand. Within days of the news more than thirty wives were concentrating their efforts on helping the widow get through the crisis. It was not an easy or pleasant task, and being in another country didn't make matters any easier but they did what they had to do to get the job done. Despite tears, fears and aching hearts, the women of the battalion gathered the courage to stifle their own concerns and care for one of their own who needed them.

ONE ACT OF KINDNESS

Sitting in my home office, a makeshift room of shelves and tables, I mused to myself out loud, "So, this is what it feels like to finally lose your mind." I had just finished a ten-minute tirade of shouting to the walls, yelling at the cat and dog, and generally grabbing and tearing any useless piece of paper I could find into confetti. This mental lapse had ended with me tilting my head back to its farthest reach on my shoulders and shouting to the faceless higher power in the heavens, "How much more do you want me to take on, Lord? I'm at my wits' end here and could really use an answer!"

And then they came...the tears that had welled up inside during countless deployment briefings, endless meetings and telephone calls from other spouses, friends and family in crisis at all hours of the day and night. My body shook with a fierceness as the tense muscles between my shoulders fired up once again—a reminder of the stress that had silently built up inside me over the previous six months. I felt tired, exhausted—so tired that even my hair hurt. What more could I do? How much more was to be asked of me?

As the flow of tears subsided, and the body began to regain control of the internal earthquake that was shaking it from head to toe, I collapsed once again into my old but comfortable work chair. Running my fingers through my hair, massaging my scalp from front to back, it became apparent that an answer was not forthcoming any time soon, at least not one that would be immediately obvious.

Just then the phone rang and I thought to myself, *God, if this is one more person who needs me to do something I think I'll just lose it.* Reluctantly I picked up the receiver and rendered my standard greeting. Kate, a respected and trusted, although new, friend was on the other end of the line. "Hey, girl, what can I do for you," I asked, hoping that the need was going to be simple or at least short.

"Nothing really," she said. "I was just thinking about you and thought about how many times we call and ask you for help and advice when it occurred to me that we never ask how you are doing or if you need anything. So I thought I'd call and ask. How are you doing?"

Somewhere, deep inside, I started to laugh and a wonderful feeling began to traverse its way through my entire being. A small smile broadened across my face and grew with each word she spoke. The fire in my muscles began to subside and the stone in my heart began to get smaller and smaller until it felt like a pebble you'd find among the sands on the beach. I told Kate that I was fine and that I really appreciated her calling, that it was nice to have someone ask. She didn't ask for anything that day, instead she was the help and support, the answer I had begged God for earlier.

HONORS TO THE FLAG

The military has been a part of my life since before birth. Born into an Air Force family I first experienced the military through the eyes of a child. It never occurred to me that there were children in the world who did not stop at the sound of the 5 p.m. cannon announcing the lowering of the flag. In fact, it was practically a sin not to stop, face the direction of the post headquarters where Old Glory flew, place my right hand over my heart and wait as the sounds of "Colors" rang through the massive public address speakers positioned throughout Fort Hamilton, Wheelus Air Force Base, and any other base we were assigned to at that time. People, on foot or in cars, dotted the countryside as they halted what they were doing, even those playing sports, and paid honors to the flag of our nation.

Even in our movie theaters, before any feature was allowed to start, the national anthem bellowed throughout the theater as images of the flag and the armed forces that served it, flashed across the canvas screen. Every spectator in the theater rose to his or her feet; active duty personnel stood stiff and staunch at attention while family members straightened their backs and once again placed their hands over their hearts. It was the expected and traditional thing to do.

It wasn't until I was twelve years old that I realized that not everyone pays this respect to the symbolic passing of our flag. I was visiting with a friend at Holloman Air Force Base, New Mexico, when the cannon resounded. Cheryl grabbed my arm and began tugging at me fiercely to run into the Base Exchange. "Hurry, or we'll get caught out here," she shouted.

Mildly confused, I relented to her feverish pulling on my shirtsleeve and darted into the overhang of the store. "What is wrong with you? Why did you run so hard? It's only 'Colors,'" I blurted.

"Yeah, I know," she said, "but I hate standing out on the street looking like a nerd when everyone else avoids it like the plague."

Too often now, thirty-five years later, I realize how my friend felt, and just how many others share this sentiment. I have watched as people leaving from work, time their departure to be either before or after the flag comes down. I have actually watched as men and women, some in uniform, some not, hearing the music, continue to walk, work, talk and drive, seemingly ignorant of the symbolism of the sounds they are hearing. Maybe I am a dinosaur, a relic of a history and tradition long outdated, but I still stop, my children stop and their children are learning to stop and render honors as well. It saddens me that so many others do not.

Even now, with the passage of the anniversary of the World Trade Center tragedy, the intensity has faded and the flag passes by unacknowledged by spectators who do not rise, raise their hand or uncover their heads. It is not the symbol of our nation that demands the respect but the thousands of men and women, sons and daughters, husbands and wives, who serve every day to protect it, who suffer and sacrifice for it, that should be given that one moment of honor.

EVERYBODY IS A HERO

Everybody has a hero, especially in the chaos of today's world. We all need someone we can look to for guidance, strength, and hope. Heroes are not the multi-million or billionaires who donate freely to charities, colleges, medical causes and orphanages—that's philanthropy; it's also a pretty smart tax move. The wonderful thing about heroes is that most people don't see themselves as one—at least not until someone points it out to them. Those are the best heroes of all—the quiet, reserved, even withdrawn figure in the back of a room, who stepped forward on one occasion to stand up against an injustice, to offer words of comfort to a sad heart; the man who had four dollars to his name and gave three to a homeless family on the street; the woman who invites a family of four, living in a shelter, to dinner at her small and overcrowded home, when she can barely feed the four occupants there already.

It was 1956, and while the world was not at war, it was definitely on the move. The Air Force was sending people to Wheelus Air Force Base in Tripoli, North Africa, for special assignments. Jane's husband had left for Tripoli three months before her and when news came that he had arranged for a place to stay and passage for her and their three young children, Jane's heart soared. When she reported to the transportation office, the airman on duty advised Jane that she and her family would be Africa-bound by ship in seven days.

Armed with only the burning desire to reunite her family, Jane fired through the paperwork involved in passports, travel documents, household good shipping and countless shots that had to be taken. Undaunted by the insurmountable tasks that lay ahead, the twenty-four-year-old mother of three pushed forward and boarded the ship one week later, carrying one infant, a diaper bag, one suitcase and dragging two protesting toddlers behind. A young sailor saw Jane struggling with the bags and children and gathered up her things, forging a way through the now increasing mass of servicemen and other travelers, helped her to find her small cabin room, and then disappeared once again into the galley way. That was Jane's hero for the day.

Ten days and a million frazzled nerves later, the young Air Force wife emerged from her ship's cabin to face the first dry land she had seen in over a week. Confronted with arid desert lands, coconut trees and an overwhelming sense of anxiety, Jane and her "child" crew trudged down the ramp, searching through the mass of uniforms and turbans for the tall, dark-haired man that was her husband. Finding him at last she struggled through the maze of people, all but collapsing into his arms. "I can't believe you're finally here," he whispered.

With a hoarse voice, fighting through the tears, she replied quietly, "Where else would I be?"

SISTERHOOD

There is a special kind of bond that develops between women who are married to the military. These women are joined together by a mutual love for their husbands and dedication to the lifestyle they lead. It promotes an internal strength of caring and sharing. These silent soldiers share the same fears, the same lives and the same loneliness.

Many outsiders view this relationship as a clique of sorts but it is more than that—it is the tie essential to the survival of women during multiple field exercises, deployments, late night "war watches" and sole parenting. It is a bond that is uncommon in any other walk of life.

Lacking in the stability of a "one place, one home" lifestyle, these ladies are drawn to each other out of need, concern and a willingness to help each other. They become the missing sisters, mothers, and friends who were left at home.

Occasionally these bonds last only for the

duration of their stay at each new military base, or end at the termination of a deployment and the return to "normal routines." But, in most cases they become a deep, durable, almost familial relationship. These are the bonds that carry military wives through the hard times, joys and sorrows.

THINGS NOT TO SAY TO A MILITARY SPOUSE

I guess you're used to him being gone by now—it must be easy for you.
(It's never easy—you just get better at it.)

That's why you get all that extra money and free housing too....
(What extra money? And I pay for my housing with my taxes, lower income and service.)

You knew your life would be like this when you married the military....
(Had an idea, but really didn't know because I've never been married to the military before....)

Well, it's not as if you are in the military....
(Might as well be...)

Hey, at least your husband has a job....
(It's not a job—it's a profession.)

Don't you just love all the travel?
(Yeah, and the packing, unpacking, broken/lost furniture, changing phone numbers, address book modifications, chaos, etc. Get the idea?)

Don't you wish you could just have a normal life?
(This isn't normal?)

No way I'd let my husband go live in the desert with a bunch of women. You know how things can happen.
(Thanks for calming my nerves—never thought of that before.)

You are so lucky—my husband never goes anywhere—he's always underfoot and on my nerves.
(Okay, I'll trade you—your husband goes, mine stays.)

I think the soldiers should just refuse to fight and come home...(Great idea—Let's hope they don't do that if we're ever attacked at home)

My husband's job is just as dangerous as your husband's.

(Oh, people shoot at him and blow up things around him on a daily basis too?)

Aren't you proud of your Soldier?

(Nah—now my '68 Mustang—that I'm proud of.)

Doesn't it bother you that he/she could get killed?

(Oh my Lord—that thought never entered my mind! Now I'm really scared. Thanks for bringing it to my attention!)

I'll bet your kids loved living in all those different places.

(Nope—they were kind of hoping to grow up in one place, knowing all their relatives—really makes Italy look boring, ya know.)

ALONE AND AFRAID

Krys lay on the wooden patio steps to her modular home, weeping into the weathered grain of the stairs as the heavy rains pelted her skin. Her thin, broad shoulders shook with each emotional spasm that racked her body all the way down to her feet. Surveying the black-and-blue blotches that were rapidly swelling around the bottom of her leg, it was becoming painfully obvious that she had broken one, if not more, of the bones in her foot and ankle. She searched desperately for something to reach the cordless phone that had flown from her hands as she tumbled down the back stairs of her home. Just inches out of her reach, Krys had twisted and turned as much as the pain would allow her to reach the one instrument that could bring help. Alone, afraid, wet, and in extreme pain she grabbed the one side rail of the steps and dragged herself closer to the phone.

Fighting back the feelings of fear and

helplessness, she pulled the phone closer to her, one fingertip at a time, until it was nestled in the palm of her hand. Krys quickly dialed the number, not to 9-1-1, not even to the military hospital, but to the home of someone she knew and trusted to help her. Within minutes, Sam and her husband were at the house, stabilizing Krys on the porch while talking to the emergency room on the phone.

Weeks later, after Krys was on the mend, someone asked her why she hadn't called the emergency service people in her town. Her response was swift and short. She called the people she trusted—the ones she knew would be there for her.

STRENGTH FROM WITHIN

In the military community you meet a lot of people from a variety of lifestyles and beliefs. But every once in a while you meet a wife who is truly inspiring—just by living life.

Linda was diagnosed with colon cancer during yet another deployment of her husband's unit. Word spread quickly through the military Family Readiness Group of her ailment. Everyone she knew made offers of meals, driving assistance, childcare and housekeeping. Staunchly and without reservation, Linda graciously thanked all the callers and simply answered that she would be all right and would call if she needed help.

It took almost a week to get her husband back home, but she persevered, insisting all the while that she was fine and did not want to impose on the other families.

Immediately after surgery the wives of her husband's unit began stopping by to check on her at the hospital. Still weak from the surgery, Linda greeted every visitor with a positive image and promising smile. Losing twenty pounds in less than two weeks, and a major part of her colon did nothing to dampen her bright light and positive nature. "I'll be back on my feet before you know it," she told me during one visit…and she was and still is—but then there never was any real doubt of any other possible outcome. Linda, like so many other women who face crisis after crisis, separation and despair, climbed out of the abyss that threatened to swallow her, struggled to the top of her mountain, raised her arms to the heavens and came down triumphant. Even after a second recurrence of the cancer Linda is still active, volunteering to help with anything, attending meetings and functions and continues to be a major inspiration to the women of her group and just about anywhere.

HOW DO YOU DO IT?

I have met with many civilian wives who have confronted me with the typical response when they learn that my husband has been deployed twenty-seven times in twenty-six years. "How can you do this time after time?" "I couldn't bear to have my husband gone that long." "Don't know how you manage to do this again and again." The real truth is sometimes we don't handle it—we get mad, we cry, we scream at the empty side of our bed, beating the pillow (as if this will help), cursing and vowing that this will be the "last time" we do this. Anger and frustration build up to such a peak that it seems almost unbearable.

We know deep in our hearts that if the car has one more trip to the shop, if the kids get into one more foolish squabble, if the lawnmower won't start (again), if the cat runs away or the dog dies—that will be it—all traces of sanity, rational and logical function will be abandoned—just as abandoned as we feel we are.

And then there comes the call, the letter, the e-mail, from a brother in California or a sister in Arizona or a friend in Georgia who takes the time to remember that you are alone and may just need to hear a friendly voice. Some days that is all you need to get through until tomorrow.

WE HAVE SOME OF THE STRANGEST DAYS

Marian has been a loyal and steadfast friend. The first time we met it was brief, friendly and typical of two military wives exchanging information. Marion had lived in Heidelberg for many years and was a wealth of knowledge. But the second time we met was a whole other story...

I was walking down the hallway to the ACS office when I noticed a tall, thin man dressed all in black, with a large backpack strapped to his shoulder, leaving the men's room across the hall from the credit union. His outfit looked like that of someone preparing to go mountain climbing and seemed a little odd for the cool, but not cold, German climate.

I glanced briefly into the credit union, just out of curiosity, only to see the man, now with a ski mask covering his face, pointing a large knife at one of the tellers behind the counter. I walked, swiftly and calmly, the remaining thirty feet to the ACS office, closed the door and whispered to Marian that she needed to call the military police as someone was robbing the credit union.

Still in disbelief, Marion passed the information to the desk Sergeant on the phone. Watching out the door, concentrating on the credit union exit to make sure that the thief had not left the building, I prayed fervently for the young woman who was being threatened and hoped that the man would not hurt her.

After many anxious minutes the tall, sleek man ran out of the credit union, full backpack tossed across his shoulders, and bolted down the stairs. I ran to the railing and yelled down to the soldiers below, "Stop that man—he just robbed the credit union!" I can only imagine how unbelievable it must have sounded to the people on the stairs—like something out of an old western television show. But one young Army Specialist must have seen the seriousness in my eyes or heard the panic in my voice as he turned and pursued the thief, enlisting the aid of another man. They chased the robber for more than a mile when they finally caught him, subduing him until the Military Police arrived.

I spent the next three hours repeating the story of

what I had seen and done to various criminal investigators and police officers while the suspect was booked and taken to jail.

My friend Marian and I still muse over the events of that day and realize that it was actually one more example of how often the military wife is overlooked. The two young men who chased the robber down were given heroes' coverage in the newspapers and military television broadcasts as having saved the credit union more than $20,000 dollars and each was rewarded with awards and cash as thanks for their actions. I was, and remain to this day, "the unidentified housewife who sounded the alarm."

THE AFTERMATH OF 9/11

As a freelance writer for military newspapers I am often awestruck by some of the people I encounter and the impact they have, not just on the soldiers and families but the world in general. CSM Frank Plass was just one of them.

CSM PLASS AND THE FLAG
(Frank Plass is not a military spouse, but his story deserves telling.)

Patriots and heroes continue to emerge from the ashes of this nation's greatest tragedy. Joined in a common bond, they work tirelessly to help those injured and in need. Citizens across the country raise their hands to offer to help in any way possible. Candles are lit in silent memoriam and American flags fly from buildings, cars, bicycles and homes in a dynamic display of unification. Phone calls flooded the crisis lines asking but one question, "What can I do to help?"

Command Sergeant Major (Ret.) Frank Plass found his answer while watching a television broadcast from his home in Harris County. "Help Heal America," was auctioning flags and other items raise funds for the Red Cross. Plass, who is also the Honorary Regimental Command Sergeant Major, 29th Infantry Regiment, grabbed his American flag out of its casing and headed for the fundraiser.

The flag had flown over the 29th Infantry Regiment Headquarters until it was presented to Plass on the day of his retirement in 1971. It didn't occur to him until he was halfway to the telethon that he would never see that flag again. Plass is a thirty-three-year military veteran of World War II, Europe and Pacific, the Korean War, and the Vietnam War. The colors were retired and given to him at his retirement. He said that when they presented him that flag—it was one of the proudest days of his life. But he thought he could help others, not as fortunate as he, by letting the flag be auctioned off. He knew in heart he was doing a good thing.

When he arrived at the telethon he gave the flag to the Red Cross worker and told her its history. He told her that he was donating it on behalf of himself and the 29th Infantry Regiment. Two people at the auction heard the story and decided that his sacrifice was too great to make. Gathering their funds and friends together they bid $1,000 for the flag. Winning the bid, they gathered up their full muster, precious cargo in hand and hunted the parking lot for the Soldier who donated it.

Plass was still sitting in his truck, convincing himself that he had done the right thing. The young auction winners found him, and despite his insistence that they keep the flag, returned the flag to the aged warrior and thanked him for his years of service. A grateful and deeply touched Soldier was so moved that he had to wait several minutes before returning home. The young woman who had placed the winning bid told me later that "Meeting this man, seeing the sacrifice he was willing to make, was the most memorable part of today for me and one of those memories that I will carry with me always. He truly symbolizes what this country is all about."

As I was preparing my story for the local military paper, I asked him why he had made such a potentially emotional sacrifice. Frank drew up his chest, squared his shoulders and with the stern, weathered face of a career Soldier quietly said that his country, his Army, took care of him and his family for over thirty-three years. It was his honor to give something back.

AND OH, THE SCANDALS…

The news media, print and broadcast, are filled daily with reports of some military person accused of "conduct unbecoming," some Soldier returning from the war creating havoc with his family, shooting up the neighborhood or even more dominant in the news, the stories of military spouses cheating, leaving their husbands and wives, falling victims to the long time apart. Studies are conducted, panels are formed and psychologists delve into the psyche of soldiering and war to identify just what causes these crises to occur. Well there's a no-brainer—it's called life, life under the watchful eye of America, examined by counselors, specialists and all-knowing experts who can tell anyone just what causes military personnel and their families to behave so scandalously.

What they don't study or report is that for every moment of gossip, scandal and bad behavior, there are hundreds of moments of trust, faith and courage. For every Soldier who falls victim to the harshness of war, there are thousands who just make it from one day to another, thanking their God to be home safely. For every spouse who abandons their Soldier and his or her military way of life, there are countless numbers of those who hold true to the course, write the letters, wave the flags and flood with tears when their Soldier returns home safely. I doubt there will ever be a study done to find out why that happens, but they don't need to really—we call it commitment, we call it duty, we call it love.

YOU KNOW YOU'RE A MILITARY WIFE IF:

Boxes and furniture in your home still bear orange, blue or green stickers with inventory numbers on them, and you don't notice them until you're moving again.

Your children refer to their home as their current duty station or quarters.

Your cupboard or baker's rack is filled with cookbooks written by other military wives and recipes prepared in three other countries.

Your coffee table books include among them title such as *Life at Fort Stewart, Getting Around Poland,* and *The Army Wife Manual.*

None of your furniture matches any other piece in your home.

Your walls have little houses on them filled with shot glasses from Germany, Italy, Spain, Georgia, Colorado and California—to name a few.

Your refrigerator is magnet heaven.

Your job resume indicates that you are someone who can't hold a job for more than 2.5 years.

Your photo albums don't have names like "Vacation at Grandma's" or "Our trip to the lake," but titles like "Fort Carson 1982-1985," "Germany 1988-1991," and "Mark's Gulf War Memories."

Your home is filled with crystal from Czechoslovakia, baskets from Italy, steins from Germany and pottery from Poland.

You wish they would dedicate a television series to decorating military quarters.

You can convert miles into kilometers in your head.

You don't go for a stroll—you volksmarch.

You don't have knick-knacks—you have chatchki.

None of your children were born in the same state.

You refer to the time you lived in any one place as "our tour in..."

Your dog is from Georgia, your cat is from California and your car is from Texas.

Your child's passport has more stamps than the local post office.

Your family pictures include the Eiffel Tower, Tower of London and German castles, but you've never seen the Grand Canyon or Statue of Liberty.

Your child's essays on "What I Did on My Summer Vacation" for the last four years includes packing and moving somewhere.

You refer to your furniture as your household goods.

Your luggage is commonly referred to as your "hold baggage."

You know the best places to shop in seven different states and three countries.

Your child has yearbooks from three different high schools.

When someone tells you they are from a certain state you immediately try to identify what military base is located there.

Your grocery store is called a commissary.

News stories and articles about soldiers make you misty.

You speak in acronyms (PCS, ETS, LES, TDY, NCOER, OWC, to name a few).

Your child acts up in the grocery store and you tell them to "drop and give me ten."

In your head and heart are the memories of a
lifetime spent living, not just existing.

THE REUNION—WHEN YOUR SOLDIER RETURNS

Even after all the deployments and time apart, there remains one real and true fact—the only thing harder than sending your Soldier away…is bringing them back home. Every deployment is different and impacts families differently. For soldiers who have been in the military more than ten years the scenario has changed from search and destroy to secure and maintain, evolving finally to make nice with the people you were blowing up three years ago. How can it not directly impact the Soldier and the family?

From the day they ship out until the moment we see their faces filing through a gymnasium door, unloading off a bus, standing only yards away in a full formation, we plan for their return. More often than not those reunions are a far cry from our plans. My first reunion I thought my guy would just love the fact that I had lost twenty pounds, bought a new dress and made special dinner arrangements for that day. I snickered as I thought to myself, *I'll be lucky to get out of the parking lot.* I was right, he fell asleep in the car before we left the lot.

Jessica planned for the quiet time, letting her Soldier rest, not making any plans for family gatherings and making sure that the kids knew Daddy might be a little too tired the first day to play. Proud of all the arrangements she had made, all the training and briefings she had attended, the notes she had taken to insure that her reunion would be just right, leaving nothing to chance...except the mother, father, three brothers, grandmother, grandfather and great-aunt who "surprised" her at the reunion site to help her welcome her Soldier home.

Monika bought the "naughty nightie," chilled the wine, lit the fireplace and put the kids up with her best friend for the night. She arrived at the welcome home site, dressed to the nines, her newly purchased cologne wafting through the gym. She hugged her Soldier tightly, mylar balloons with "Welcome Home, Hero" floating on the ribbons attached to the yellow roses she had bought fresh just hours before. Driving home she could barely contain her excitement at what she knew was going to be a glorious night. Her Soldier walked into the house, grabbed a shower, kissed her gently, grabbed a beer out of the fridge and slumped into the recliner with the remote control.

Some things just aren't what we plan them to be....

THE STRANGER
IN MY HOME

As a trainer and briefer, I have tried to prepare soldiers and spouses for the changes in their lives when a Soldier returns from deployment. It's never easy readjusting to family life with the Soldier home. Returning from the combat zone to friendly territory is fraught with trials and tribulations for many soldiers and families. Soldiers left home as Daddy bear, little Billy Bob from Mel High, Snuggle bunny, and returned as seasoned combat veterans who have witnessed crises and challenges we can only imagine. Anxiety runs rampant in many military homes just prior to the return. Some major factors include:

Return home parades and parties—why does everyone think that soldiers want loud parties with fireworks? Don't be surprised if you Soldier jumps under the table calling for cover when the fireworks go off.

Driving is a major experience. Rolling down the road to Grandma's house you see a vehicle stopped on the side of the road and move to pull over. Your Soldier grabs the steering wheel and pushes the car into the far left lane. You saw a person in need of help—your Soldier saw a roadside bomb waiting to go off.

Even going into the house can be a challenge. Your Soldier has lived in a world of everything in its place, knowing that if one thing has been moved, his or her area has been violated. Then bam! Into the house, squeaky toys decorate the living room floor, toiletries spread from one of the bathroom sink to the other, and the bathroom is inside the house!

Even the manner in which they speak changes. One counselor told me that my Soldier had changed and might be loud, abrasive, vulgar in language and short on patience. I stood in protest, not believing what I was hearing and could not believe when I shouted out, "You said he was going to change! That's how he was before he left—so change him!"

There is no gauge, meter or flow chart that accurately describes or channels how a reunion is going to happen. Some soldiers change radically, some change over time, others seem not to change at all. Bringing a Soldier home and reuniting the family is not just an event, it's a process, and the more the military spouse knows about the process, the better prepared she is for the soldier's return. There is no greater tragedy for the military family than to survive months of separation only to become victims of the reunion.

SALUTE TO THE NOT-SO WEEKEND WARRIOR

Gone are the days when the National Guard and Reserve Soldier reported to monthly meetings and summer camps. With the number of National Guard and Reserve soldiers being mobilized to deploy, the concern for and from their families increases as well.

Sean, the wife of a pilot belonging to an Air Cavalry unit, worries about her husband Roy every day. "It's not easy having him gone, but the regular Army folks have a higher profile and much of the media focus on their families. But there are a lot of us out here, separated from the military installations, without real Family Readiness Groups to help us through the hard times. It's getting better but some days it's just not enough."

Christian, whose wife is a Supply Sergeant, focuses on his community and his children. "When my church learned that Sara was being mobilized, I was overwhelmed by the amount of phone calls and notes that folks in our town made to us. We were worried a lot about the money we would lose from her regular job—a lot more than she makes in the Army—but the VFW, American Legion, Church and a whole lot of other social agencies stepped up to the plate and helped us out. The Army is recognizing the challenges we face and making programs more and more available to the Guard and Reserve families to help us through the hard times. I even got free child care so I could go to work and get some away time just for me too."

While we focus on the Soldier and families deployed, let us not forget those who signed up for the short program and ended up getting to see the whole show.

ONE LAST DEPLOYMENT

You tell yourself for the umpteenth time that this is the "last one." No more will you pack up your heart and soul and send it off to protect and serve the nation. You promise your children sincerely that there will not be another Christmas missed, or a birthday without Mommy or Daddy, that there will be no more school plays missed or parent-teacher conferences attended by only one parent. You swear adamantly that you will not attend yet another pre-deployment briefing or redeployment ceremony with flags waving, smiles flashing and bands blaring patriotic songs endlessly. And then the news comes down that the unit your Soldier is attached to is deploying once again. Your heart begins to ache in a way now much too familiar to you and the tears sit at the very outer edge of your eyes, as if in a pocket, not daring to flow down the cheek and be visible. You and your Soldier cuss and discuss the ramifications of leaving the military, whether retiring or just getting out. One of you argues the financial security of staying just "one more year," while the other lays the dragon of separation on the table and the emotional costs it extracts from the family. Somewhere during all of this one, more likely both, of you will shoot out vehemently with the phrase, "You have no clue as to what it takes to do what I do!"

Late at night, after tempers have cooled, calmer heads sit down at the family table, with coffee, tea, beer, wine, whatever the drink of choice is for the evening, and the actual discussion of what needs to be done begins.

JOURNALISTS—YA GOTTA LOVE 'EM

During the first Gulf War, I was interviewed by many journalists concerning Family Support Groups and the military families' survival techniques during the deployment. I suppose the people back in the US wanted to know how the wives and children of deployed soldiers were handling the war and the separation from family friends.

During one particular interview via satellite, it became quickly and painfully obvious that the reporter was shooting for the "emotional moment," when I would either break down in tears or lash out in anger. With each more intensely intimate question I began to understand how survivors of a plane crash feel when reporters stick microphones in their face and make statements like "So, how do you feel being the only survivor out of 247 passengers?" The final question really clinched the obvious drive of the reporter to evoke some strong emotional response when he asked, "Do you miss your family in the States?" I couldn't help but smile and think to myself, *Oh yeah, right, I'm going to state on national television that I don't miss my mommy? NOT.* Eliminating all the obviously witty comebacks, I dug into the tried, traditional and true response— "Well, sir, we all miss our families—whether we are in Germany or Georgia, but we have families here and they are the closest to home that we can get. They live the same lives, share the same fears and truly understand what we endure. I couldn't pick a better or stronger family if I tried."

HOW DID YOU MEET THESE GUYS?

Lynn was a young military policewoman when she met her husband Jack at Fort Hood, Texas. Bob was a local Killeen police officer and he stopped her for a traffic violation. He met back with her at court just to "make sure she paid the fine."

Teri was an Army medic on vacation in the Colorado Rockies, when she came across Doug, trying to hobble his way down the mountain path. Skis in hand and red in the face he admitted that he had taken a painful and embarrassing spill down the hillside. Teri supported him as they made their way down to the aid station and she has been supporting him ever since.

Mark was an Advanced Individual Training (AIT) student when we met. Processing into a new duty station, I was amazed—no, absolutely blown away—to discover that my barracks was coed.

Young male soldiers came running to the curb to help the new female soldiers unload their luggage, offering to carry the bags to their new rooms, forming quick friendships. I stood, Sergeant's stripes flashing in the night like a neon "Do Not Touch" sign, waiting for my room assignment and soon found myself alone by the side of the bus. Spying a young man walking towards the barracks I called out, "Private, come here."

He turned to me, surprised and somewhat hesitant and said "Who? Me?"

"Yes you. Grab that duffel bag and show me to Room 317." We married four years later.

Michelle and Walter grew up military brats. Their families were often stationed together; they went to the same schools and had many of the same memories and friends. From the first day they can remember, they hated each other in the typical "boy hates girl, boy loves girl" mentality of teens. Michelle thought Walter was a bully and Walter firmly believed Michelle was just another addle-brained female, until Walter joined the Army and came home to visit his family, dressed to kill in his Class A uniform. They celebrate their twenty-third anniversary this year.

Marie was an active duty Sergeant, processing

into a new duty station once again. It was an overcast and windy day in Georgia and the flight from Germany had been delayed and way too long. Thoughts of the upcoming weeks of in processing, finding new places to go, meeting new people, learning a new job, crowded her thoughts. Preoccupied by the new surroundings and fumbling with baggage and processing paperwork, she stumbled over a curb, sending her luggage and papers to the four winds. Convinced that the "powers that be" had cursed her existence and sent her to the this place as punishment, she chased the flying papers across the parking lot. Several other soldiers walked past her, ignoring her plight, when one tall, young and pleasant looking Staff Sergeant bent down and handed her some of her strewn papers. "I believe these are yours," he said quietly. Helping her to gather the rest of her dumped belongings, they began to chat. His name was Chad, and now their children call him Dad.

BABIES ARRIVE
REGARDLESS

Strength, durability, discipline and resilience are but a few words to describe the military wife. Vanessa was one example of that image.

Eight months pregnant when her husband deployed to Operation Iraqi Freedom, struggling with personal and physical issues, including a bad appendix, she maintained the home front for herself and her four-year-old son while her Soldier was off in the desert.

Late one night (or I should say—early one morning) I received the call that Evelyn had presented our unit with its newest recruit, a healthy, beautiful baby girl, Nicky. Gathering up our standard "welcome baby" basket, I headed to the hospital to welcome the new addition.

I found Evelyn and baby Nicky resting quietly amid the sterile sheets, pillowcases, striped hospital gowns and disposable slippers. Nicky occupied her clear hospital basinet next to Mom. Handing Evelyn the welcome basket, I offered to make sure that transportation was available to take her and baby Nicky home when released. Evelyn smiled and said, "That's okay—I'm going home the same way I got here—in my car." Not wanting to disturb or be a bother to anyone, Evelyn, in the middle of labor, drove herself to the hospital. When I asked her why she had not called for help she stated simply, "There are others who have greater problems and needs—I didn't want to take someone's attention from those who need help more."

LETTERS FROM HOME

The concerns military spouses face on a daily basis change constantly—we grow older, smarter, wiser, more obnoxious and more resilient. How we react to the changes in our lives and concerns of our soldiers changes as well. Looking through the papers and letters that have built up over the past twenty-six years I found evidence of that change in what I had written to my Soldier—even in those I never mailed. I also found the changes in the letters I received from my Soldier. I take a look at them from time to time to remind me, when I feel at my weakest, that I have survived tougher challenges and will continue to do so.

December 1982
Dear Mom and John,
Just wanted to thank you for the "honeymoon suite" at the Mushwhip Lodge at the Grand Canyon. We arrived late but the staff was awesome and even

fed us dinner on the house. We woke to watch the sunrise over the canyon and it was glorious. Threw the bouquet and boutonniere into the canyon—hope we didn't impale any hikers with them. Have found a small, but cozy, apartment for us and am rapidly adjusting to life as a military wife. That sounds so weird after having been on active duty. I don't know how you did it, Mom—this is a whole different world for me—not quite the cakewalk I thought it would be. Think I am rapidly disappearing into the paperwork and every time I breathe I have to produce Mark's social security number, his proof of orders or his contact information. I couldn't even get the phone turned on without it. I feel like I have moved to China and should walk ten paces to the rear. This is not going well for the home team so puhleeeease—don't give me the "time to adjust" spiel. I just needed to vent today—I'll adjust tomorrow.

June 9, 1985

Hi, Honey,

Just a quick note to say I love and miss you. I can't wait for you to finish up Drill Sergeant school so you can come home. I'm beginning to think that my new Lamaze partner is the dog. He seems to notice every time the baby moves and stares at my stomach as if to say, "What—she's awake again?" The doctor says that all is well and thank heavens, only one baby this time—no twins again. Phew! Diane has been a great help and she swears that I am nesting. Every time she turns around there is something new in the house or something just cleaned—and the baby isn't due until August. Just hope that you are here to see it.

You know I understand that your job comes first but you would think that the Army would consider a baby a matter of priority. I guess they don't because they don't have to give birth—not their priority. Some days it is just more than I can understand. The Sergeant at the hospital even said, "Well you know, ma'am, this baby is gonna be born whether or not your husband is here for it." Well, duh. Why do you have to be gone so much? I always thought that having been in the military had prepared me for just about anything—man, was I ever wrong. I don't see how some women do this for twenty or more years! Nothing prepares you for life on the "dark side of the moon." Have decided that I am not having this baby until you come home so you better get here on time—please!

February 20, 1988

Well, believe it or not, the paperwork finally came through saying that Bri and I can join you in Germany. I am soooo excited about seeing you again. Seems like it has been forever. You won't believe how much our little girl has grown in three months. I tried to call the base to let you know that we are cleared to come over but the newbie Private that answered the phone didn't even have a clue who or where you were. I had to go through the post locator and found that you were in school in some town called Vilseck temporarily. Anyway—at least I know that you are still in the same country.

I desperately need to talk to you about decisions that have to be made. The letter says we can only bring 2,500 pounds of our furniture and definitely not the washer and dryer. What do you want me to store? To bring? To sell? I don't think most of the furniture will make it through three years in an Alabama storage unit and we can only bring one car. I know my choice would be to keep the Concorde but bet you want me to bring the truck. Somebody said that we could buy a "hoopdee car"— is that an actual brand name? Please call or write and let me know.

December 25, 1990

Merry Christmas, darlin'—I know that it doesn't seem like Christmas where you are, up to your elbows in dirt, dust and camel dung, but well, Merry Christmas anyway and oh, Happy New Year too. Have renewed my belief in Santa Claus (although I think he is really our babysitter, Diana). Woke up this morning to find gifts under the tree with my name on them. Can't believe that with all you had on your mind preparing to deploy that you remembered what I wanted for Christmas—aside from your being home to celebrate it with us. I am trying to remain positive about this, but it all seems so damned unfair especially since you were already in the field for 248 days this year. So much for the Commander's word that you would be home for the holidays. I know, such is the life of the military wife...blah, blah—buck up and suck up.

At least I'm not standing at the gates like some of the wives this morning who held up posters and signs protesting your going. The sad part is that their husbands didn't even go—four of our wives were right out there in front like would-be heroines—shouting at the buses as they left. What a bunch of hypocrites—since it only took their husbands fifteen years to decide that they couldn't shoot at another human being—another crock! I don't mind that they don't agree with the cause but they can count me out on the "defend and support" side of their lives. Then to top it all off, one wife whose husband refused to deploy, called me and asked me to drive her to Mannheim to visit her husband in jail—you have no idea how much I wanted to say, "Hah—you must be drugged..." But, I was good—I went halfway—drove her to the train station and put her on the right train. Some people just amaze me.

January 16, 1991

Well, lover, I know I told you that you were one behind until you got your own war but I never thought you took me seriously. You asked for it— the chance to go and prove your combat-worthiness and now you have it. We have heard through the German news about the deadline and the bombings and air raids. Tonight is the deadline and I am truly hoping that it will pass uneventfully.

I have been doing a lot of briefings for deployment and helping them prepare. My boss scared me when he told me that we had to brief a worst-case scenario of 50% loss of life—not an easy presentation to do. Several of the ladies got up and left and I can't blame them for living in denial, but one woman actually came up and slapped me dead straight! She said she wasn't going to sit and listen to me talk about her husband dying. I just looked her right in the eye and told her, "Ma'am, I understand your feelings, but my husband is deployed too and I might not have been talking about your husband ...." Write soon—I need to know you are okay.

January 17, 1991

Agnes called me last night, actually this morning, screaming into the phone, "Oh my God—they bombed Baghdad!" Had to switch to active FRG leader mode, make sure she was okay, not alone and move on to make more phone calls. God, I hope that you are okay—keep your head down and your powder dry, baby. Krys and I spent the better part of the night checking on all the other wives and finally got done around 4:30 this morning and saw no need to sleep so shared coffee and a brotchen and headed to work. Man, am I tired—had to deal with the phone calls there too. Briefings are piling up like mad, people are in a panic and my boss had that "I know—you told me so" look on his face this morning. (He never believed that your unit would deploy, let alone go to war.) I love you, I pray for you and promise me that when you come home we will never do this again.

February 14, 1991

Happy Valentine's Day, Big Dog! Wish you were here to celebrate but did spend it with 697 of your unit's wives—had a huge family day celebration to pick up the wives' morale and spirits. Job is keeping me busy, as well as planning the family day, working with Brianna at home and school, volunteering with the Family Support Group and manning the Emergency Family Action Center after duty hours. (Bri swears that we should move in there as we spend more time there than at home. She has even brought Mr. Binky in with a pillow to crash on the cot.) Had a great time on the family day—worked a lot with the journalists and television reporters covering the day—got great coverage of the wives and had a stink load of stuff donated to give away. Vendors were absolutely dynamite in donating everything for free! Hope you can come home soon because my calendar is filling up fast.

April 19, 1991

Hey hon, sorry to deliver this through the First Sergeant but needed to make sure someone was with you when you got it. Seems that there was an incident with your mom—she's okay for now, but apparently she had a pretty severe stroke last week and she's in intensive care. Matt called and wanted to know if he should send a Red Cross notice but told him that you would be forced to decide between soldiers and family—hope he made the right call. Having watched you over the past thirteen years, I know that this would be a pretty difficult decision for you and I am fairly sure what your decision would be although I don't know how well that would sit with me either. You're a Soldier and that's what comes first—I know. Will keep you up to date as much as possible. Sent this by the courier (sometimes it pays to be in good graces with the Rear Detachment bubbas) so hope that he got it to you quickly. Will know when I hear from you next, but if you get the chance to make a call—make it to your mom—she's at St. Joe's and you have the number for that. I can wait to hear from you but you need to call your mom and she needs to hear from you. I love you.

September 1992

Okay, range rider—I know you're only out in the field but there has to be a better way to stay in touch with you than by mail. I mean, my God—you're not on another planet or continent—hell, you're not even out of state. Anyway—I called the TOC to have them catch you in the desert and got the lecture about not disturbing the rotation, be back soon, maintain, only emergency situation contact, blah, blah, blah....What kind of idiot does he think I am? You're out there playing Lord of the Desert with laser guns, barbequing in the moonlight and reflecting on the greater meaning of life while I'm stuck here with one son who got busted for shoplifting a sport hat, another whose girlfriend climbed through his window at 2 a.m. and a seven-year-old daughter who has to carry an egg around for a month like its her baby. Yes, dear, I am talking about sex education in the 3d grade. The Jeep stopped running and I can't find the keys to your truck so I can drive it instead. I imagine the spare set is sitting in your office but guess who won't let me in there either. And to end the day perfectly—the cat we thought was dead is alive and back—and delivered four babies this morning right in the middle of my shoes. Next rotation I have a better idea—I'll go play Soldier in the desert—you can stay home with the kids. Yeah—love you too.

July 01, 1999

Hi there, stranger—just a quick note to let you know that all is well here and hope that the same holds true for you wherever you are. Sometimes I really hate that part—Mom asks what you are doing and I can't tell her—let alone tell her where you are doing it. Have heard rumors that you are in Kosovo/ Bosnia area but not sure. Wanted to let you in on a few happenings during your absence—biggest one being that we don't have to worry about making it to our son's wedding—they eloped. Apparently she came down on assignment and they wanted to transfer together so they got married early. I really hate that we didn't get to be there.

Your brother called and wanted to let you know that your dad is recovering well from the—now are you ready for this—Ringling Brothers water truck that ran into his car and darn near killed him. He's still in the hospital but appears to be doing well.

Have made the final arrangements for my folks to come and visit in November (know you are thrilled about having the in-laws visit) and all is set to go for their trip to Ireland. Brianna says you two have to talk—something about a boyfriend and the date for homecoming. Your arena—not mine. Love you.

November 20, 2002

Somehow I know there was something else I was supposed to be doing today other than writing you another letter—hmmmmm—ahhhh, celebrate birthday and 20th wedding anniversary. Time sure flies when you are having fun. Not to worry though—have my gift for both as rumors are flying fast and furious that the return flights will land in four days. A lot has changed during the time you have been gone and in the twenty-four years you have been in the Army. I am really glad that I got to share it with you—good times and bad. Hate that you are gone today but know that you are in my heart always. We are making it with you gone, but our world will be better once you come home. Bri's keeping me busy with all her senior class activities and I stay busy working to pay for them all (good thing you have extra cash coming in—much more expensive to be a girl in high school than when I went through). As you can tell, schedule is busy and jam-packed but if you do manage to get home soon think we can work you in on a good time slot. I love you and miss you—can we retire now and not do this anymore?

March 9, 2003

Okay—thought we agreed not to do this again. I understand that you had to go and be with the unit, I understand that your commitment is that strong, but my fun meter is pegged. The news is filled with coverage of the war, journalists are everywhere scaring the fire out of the younger wives watching the news—seeing the 3d Brigade patch floating all over the screen—imagining that the guy they are carrying off to the side is their husband. Who in their right minds let these guys in? I only hope and pray that your job does not require you to protect one of these idiots.

Know you don't have time to write, let alone call, but wanted to let you know that care packages are still coming to you—in droves—think the whole state of New Jersey adopted you and your guys courtesy of your cousin, Bill. Have heard rumors that you are low on supplies, low on food, low on morale and that the effort is failing dismally. Have also heard everything else to the reverse. History tells me that about half is true—so write and tell me which half so I know what to send—beef jerky or bullets.

Have to admit that the temper of the nation is

very good and positive—nothing like Viet Nam—
anyone even considering speaking badly about a
Soldier meets with resistance—even those who do
not support the war—support the Soldier—totally
heartening to hear and see. I promise you that when
this is all over and you and your guys come home—
you will have a welcome home like no other. You
are, always have been and continue to be my hero.
Just promise me one thing—that we will never do
this again. Have no more in me. Love you always
and ever.

15 July 2003

My dearest love,

You may think it strange—writing to you when
you are already home but, as I lay in bed this
morning watching you sleep, I felt the need to tell
you how grateful I am that you are home safe and
that we are finally heading "for the barn," and a new
life free of deployments, field exercises and being
away from each other. Our lives together under the
military "umbrella" have been truly wonderful and I
would not trade them, or the memories, for anyone
else's. It was very strange, waking to you beside me
this morning, in a wonderful way, but odd
nonetheless. Even stranger is the knowledge that

never again will I wake to find myself alone because you are off protecting a third world country or training in the field. It is a truly awesome sensation, but a frightening one as well. We have spent so many years apart that I wonder if we will be able to adjust to being together all the time. We have grown so much and changed in so many ways these past twenty-six years. We have survived the hardest of times personally and professionally and now we must survive the "best" of times. I know that it will not be easy for us learning to live together, but I also know that it will be well worth the struggle—just to be able to do as I did this morning—wake to find you sleeping next to me, your heart beating close enough for me to hear and your arm curled tightly under your head. I listened intently to every breath you took, just reveling in the fact that you were breathing at all. There is no real way to tell you just how much I love you and how very, very glad I am that you are home safe and that we will never have to do "that" again.

STRENGTH AND COURAGE

Banners, balloons and porch signs began to fill the gymnasium halls and home yards as the 3d Brigades involvement in Operation Iraqi Freedom moved towards its end. Plans for homecoming parties occupied most of the conversations in the neighborhoods of Fort Benning. Flower shops were inundated with requests for yellow roses and local craft stores could not stock enough yellow, red, white and blue paint it seemed. Our soldiers were coming home and the entire base was in celebration mode.

As the wives of the Sledgehammer Brigade reported to Kiefert Gym to finish our final decorations and banner hanging the morning of the soldiers' return, we were brought back to the reality of just how lucky we were and how strong a woman must be to be a military wife. One wife, new to the brigade, blurted, "Man, somebody took one of our spaces for the banners," and moved forward to remove it to another spot. Another wife, not so new, grasped her by the arm and said softly—"It stays—right there for everyone to see." The banner was blazing with red, white and blue letters with the words, "Welcome Home Sledgehammer Soldiers—We love you!" The signatures of the banner makers, in red, white and blue glitter, captured the fluorescent lights of the gym, shining like a thousand tiny stars. The family, not wanting to make a fuss, but wanting to show their support for the returning soldiers, had hung the banner in the dark of the night before their scheduled return. It hung there, a testimony to the true courage that it takes to be a military wife, so all who came would know that soldiers were still ever present in their hearts. All of us who knew the family that had hung the banner were humbled by her strength and devotion to soldiers. Our friend and fellow military wife would not be greeting her Soldier with the rest—he fell on the battlefield in Iraq.

YOU'RE SO LUCKY

Colorful and booming fireworks illuminated the Anniston, Alabama, sky where Elizabeth and her two children had gathered to celebrate the 4th of July. Open to both military and civilian families, the event offered the opportunity for both sides of the "world" to meet and mingle and share stories. One young woman sat in awe as Elizabeth spoke of her travels in Europe and across the United States. "How exciting it must be for you, to travel so much and see so many new and exciting places. I've never been outside of Alabama. My family all lives here and has forever. I can't go around the corner without bumping into someone who knows my whole family. Nothing exciting or new ever happens here. It's always the same old dull stuff. I would love to live your life."

Elizabeth turned to her and quietly said, "Yes, and there are many days when I would love to live yours."

THE MILITARY CHILD

Give praise to the military child for as strong and flexible as their parents are, they are possibly even more so. They adjust as frequently, yet with more flexibility than we. They move from state to state, country to country, with little or no choice or voice and yet manage to build and rebuild their circle of friends ever again. They stand to the side, often with their mothers and even more so not, while the accolades of their Soldier parent are paraded before them. Too many times they are posed with the question, "You must be so proud of your dad and what he does."

It is not often that they are recognized or rewarded for their sacrifices and the adjustments they make in their lives.

The military child:

Can identify another military child with ease.

Moves from one school to another, restarting in sports, club activities and special classes with frequent regularity and yet tries out for those activities all over again.

Can normally speak one if not more foreign languages (at least enough to go shopping).

Understands the differences in world cultures, not just cities and states of the US.

Navigates the streets and metro systems of Europe just as easily as they drive a bicycle in Colorado Springs.

Steps in at special functions for their kid brother or sister when Dad or Mom is not able to do so.

Holds the hand of their baby sister while walking her to her first day at a new school because Dad isn't able to do so.

Knows what it means always to be the new kid at school.

Says the Pledge of Allegiance with heart and soul, because it is their way of life.

Will stand and defend the weaker, new kids at their school or base because they have "been there, done that."

Grows up faster because they must.

Usually has yearbooks from two or three different high schools.

Discovers early on the value of e-mail and web pages as a means of learning about new places and staying in touch with old friends.

WHEN THE MILITARY CHILD BECOMES THE SOLDIER

When we marry a member of the Armed Forces, whether Army, Navy, Air Force, Marine or Coast Guard, we realize that there will inevitably be a time when our spouse will deploy, ship out or be stationed in a dangerous area or combat zone. We prepare for it mentally, we talk to other spouses about it, and we attend briefings and seminars to help us get ready for the day. We talk to our children about it to help them understand why their mom or dad must go away again. Years of separation have seasoned us, matured us and taught us how to be strong during these times. Over those years our children have grown up. Many have moved away and because of their upbringing and close association with the military, many more are now serving in the military themselves.

And a new chapter begins—the chapter of Military Mom. It is one thing to send your adult spouse off to do battle, but nothing prepares you for standing on the same field you stood on just months before, sending off yet another part of your heart into harm's way. As my son boarded the bus that would take him to the airfield, I held him close, told him I would miss him and pray for him and reminded him to look up his dad when he got to Iraq. I thought I was alone in my sorrow until I heard some of the other moms and wives say much the same thing..."If you get a chance to get to FOB Falcon, tell your father I miss him," "Remember your mom is at Camp Virginia—try to hook up with her while you're there," "Your brother knows you are coming and will try to catch up with you when you arrive," "Give your dad a hug for me when you see him, okay?" And again, we watch, we weep, we pray, and add one more blue star to the windows of our homes and cars, and tie one more yellow ribbon to the post in our front yard. Tell me again how being married to the military is not so different from other lives?

BLUE STAR FAMILIES

With all the new programs, terminology and acronyms that have emerged from the changing face of the Army and Army Family programs, you might think that the last thing we need is one more "targeted or labeled" group of military family members, but this group definitely bears recognition and often gets little or none.

Blue Star families are the mothers, fathers, grandparents, sons and daughters, sisters and brothers, unknown to most, but a valuable source of support, care and love to many soldiers. You will often find them writing letters to lonely soldiers, sending care packages full of cakes, cookies and beef jerky. They are the aunts and uncles raising their sister or brother's children because of the deployment. They are the school teacher who foster-parents a soldier's dog because the only other option was to take her to the pound. They are an individual, a team, a community full of pride—a pride that began many decades ago when a small group of mothers gathered in a little-known Michigan town and has evolved into a global organization. Populated by mothers, the Blue Star Mothers of America, Inc. was born in 1942.

Today the concept remains the same but the audience has a greater reach and impact on our society. Flags with one, two sometimes as many as three blue stars hang proudly in homes of families of American soldiers performing their duty. We see them everywhere—at rallies, at airports, at welcome-home and other ceremonies. These are the self-sacrificing volunteers who willingly dragged themselves out of their warm, dry beds at 2 a.m. to stand in a freezing cold hanger in Bangor, Maine, banners hung high, hand-held flags flapping in the breeze to hug, thank and welcome home soldiers as they shifted from one aircraft to another. Hot chocolate, coffee, and pastries flowed freely along with the hundreds of "thank you for your service" calls. (No Soldier went unhugged, unwelcomed—that was the report my husband gave me.) They are usually the ones we walk past, scratching our heads and quizzically asking, "Who are all those crazy old coots anyway?"

That answer is easy—they are the Blue Star

Families—whose son sleeps in a cave in Afghanistan, whose niece walks patrol in Fallujah, whose brother provides medical care in Kosovo. They are one of the new silent majorities whose voice is beginning to echo from coast to coast and across the globe. And the message is clear—causes be damned—we support our soldiers!

CHARITY'S BIRTHDAY

Charity was running around the parade field at a 4th of July party, giggling and jumping like any other five-year-old little girl. "Today is my birthday," she announced to anyone who would listen, "and these fireworks are just for me cuz it's my special day." Her good humor continued well into the first hours of the celebration but waned when she saw her school friend, Melissa, walking the grounds with her dad. Charity's father, a Ranger, was in Afghanistan, part of a small group of volunteers who had gone on special assignment. Sadness filled her eyes as she began to wish her daddy could be there too.

When her grandmother saw the change in Charity's face, she walked over to a Soldier on the field and whispered in his ear. The young Soldier, a fellow Ranger, walked over to Charity and said, "I know I'm not your dad, but can I fill in for him today in wishing you a happy birthday?" Charity's heart lightened as the Ranger gave her a hug and kiss and said, "That's from your dad just for you." The grateful grandmother hugged the Ranger and he walked back to his fellow soldiers across the field. Moments later an entire platoon of Rangers gathered in front of the blanket where Charity and her grandmother waited for the fireworks to begin. Taking a knee in front of the two, the platoon gathered together and broke out into a rousing, though off-key, chorus of "Happy Birthday" and everyone within hearing distance joined in the song. When they were done singing, one by one the soldiers gave the once again jubilant Charity a hug and kiss and said, "That's from your dad—just for you." The fireworks couldn't hold a candle to the light from Charity's smile that night.

WALKING TO KUWAIT

Karen's husband had deployed on a lengthy exercise to the deserts of Kuwait for what would be an "undefined period of time." Her home was decorated with yellow ribbons, like the homes of most of her neighbors. She attended the Family Readiness Group meetings, boxed and shipped care packages, wrote letters of support and did what she could do to occupy her mind and time while her Soldier was gone. But it never seemed to be enough. She wanted to do something that would really let her Soldier know how much she supported him.

Every day Karen and her neighbors would gather for an early morning stroll around their housing area. An idea began to form in Karen's mind and within days she knew what she could do...she would walk to Kuwait! Navigating the internet and determining the estimated distance from her home to the New Jersey Kabal where her Soldier was living, Karen put together a plan to "virtually" walk the 7,902 miles that would take her to her husband.

Sharing her plan with another soldier's wife, the idea spread quickly through the company group and other wives became interested. A plan was made, a date was set. August 1, 2002, Karen and thirty-six other wives met and set off on a symbolic one-mile walk to start their trek. Local newspapers and television stations had heard of the groups plan and spread the word through the media.

What began as one woman wanting to show support rapidly spread through families and friends and became a monument to their soldiers. More than 187 family members, volunteers and friends, blazed the trail with t-shirts and sweatshirts announcing their "Virtual Walk to Kuwait" project. From New Jersey to California, e-mails came weekly with new volunteers donating their miles to help Karen accomplish her goal. A motorcycle club in Atlanta parked their bikes on Labor Day and walked a combined total of 100 miles for her. A group of joggers in Oklahoma donated 150 miles. Parents, grandparents, friends and strangers heard of the project, and volunteered to join the cause. A bicycle club in Florida donated more than 200 miles. A young woman in Indiana, who was walking for cancer research donated her miles to the group as well.

Tracking of the project was done in miles and milestones. As miles were turned in each week, e-mails were sent announcing the progress of the group. Each notice announced a new city or country. "We reached Atlanta today!" "New York is ours!" "We're paddling our way across the Atlantic—man, is the water cold." "Today we saw the city of Cairo!" "Tomorrow we take Kuwait!"

On November 11, 2002, the group met once more at the Infantry memorial on Fort Benning to finish their walk. Once again the media gathered to cover the event. As young and old, two- and four-legged, stroller-pushing and stroller-riding participants gathered to end their trek, they paused for a moment and said a prayer for their soldiers who were not there. With the last mile, the group had amassed 11,470 miles total—to Kuwait and halfway home. Karen said to a reporter, "Somehow that just seems right—now the guys only have to make it the rest of the way home."

ADVICE TO THE NEW MILITARY WIFE FROM AN OLD ONE

Semper Gumby—remain flexible always—elastic versus plastic (if this makes no sense to you—trust me—it will later).

Maintain your individuality—make a life for yourself as well as for your marriage.

Get to know your whole community—not just the military side of it—it will help you out in the hard times.

Learn the hard lessons first and fast—you'll know which ones they are.

Rumors are worth what you pay for them.

Develop and grow in your own right—not just the light of your Soldier.

Patience, patience, patience.

Hold your friends close—but your enemies even closer—and yes—you will make a few.

Remember you married the man *and the uniform*—even though you will swear countless times you did not.

Remember WHY you married the Soldier.

Continue to renew your relationship with each other—go out on a date every six months or so.

There is no officer or enlisted spouse—just the person who is married to an officer or enlisted Soldier.

Remember all that you have seen, done and survived and share it with those who come after you, that they may grow from your experience.

Understand that you may be his wife, but the military is his way of life—adapt, adjust and overcome—resistance is futile.

The life of a military wife is not easy, but you get better at it and become a better person for it.

THE STRENGTH IN THOSE I HAVE MET

Throughout the years, twenty-six actually, that I have roamed the globe with my Soldier I have had the honor and privilege of meeting many other wives and husbands of soldiers. Some were strong, others were not; some were flexible, some were not; many possessed the same commitment and dedication to their Soldier as I did, few did not; some were wives of the military, others were military wives. Why distinguish between the two? Because the difference is real—especially for those who have earned the title of Military Wife.

There are those who marry a Soldier believing that their Soldier serves the military, they don't. Some believe that it is not their call to duty that drives their lives; a military wife knows that call to duty is her responsibility also. One will not be as flexible, will not understand the total involvement she has in supporting her Soldier; the other does it without thinking. A military wife believes, lives the life of long separations, sole parenting, and tough choices that have to be made without thought, without complaint. She is the military wife, she lives in the shadows, accepts the radical changes, works with what she has to make home and family more than just words. Tears flow freely down her cheeks when she stands, hand over heart as the flag is lowered daily. Her breathing is shallow and her heart aches each time she attends a memorial service or hears taps play. For this is the life she chooses to adapt to, the life she accepts because it is the life of her Soldier and to live without him in her life is not an option.

HEADING FOR
THE "BARN"

Remembering back to the very first retirement ceremony I had attended, I mused at the way I felt about it then and how I feel about it now. Ceremonies have changed now and spouses are recognized, and awarded, with their Soldier for their dedication and sacrifice. Walking across the stage, back straight, and tears held in abeyance, memories of hard times and good times, old friends and new, flashed through my mind. Leaving this way of life behind us will not be easy, but it is yet another adjustment that we will make. As we turned the corner and stepped off the stage, I realized that while we are leaving behind the uniforms, duffel bags, TA-50 and packing tape, we are also taking with us years of memories, of battles waged and won, lives lived in a culture and environment unlike those of many of our family and friends. Nothing can replace the years we shared with the soldiers and families of the Army, nor would I want them to.

But, as happens with all old soldiers and old spouses, we move on once again. Never to pack again (hopefully), to set down roots, finally attend family events and watch the plants that we put into the ground grow, retire for the season and come back again in the same place next year. Like those plants, we will finally find our permanent place, where we will look at old photo albums, remember old friends and truly miss these days of our lives now past. Our greatest adventure is yet before us.

And then you retire....

For twenty or more years your entire world focuses on the military. You wake up every morning to the sound of reveille, the last chords of taps waft through the air of your current duty station as you drift off to sleep. You shop at the commissary and post exchange, receive your medical care at a Military Medical Treatment Facility (MTF) and your children attend Department of Defense (DoDDS) schools.

Routinely you attend at least one Family

Readiness Group (FRG) meeting or briefing monthly dealing with the deployment of your Soldier. You pack and unpack your household goods (civilian equivalent—your "stuff") four or more times and you memorize the local hospital, dental, public works and emergency numbers of each new duty station (civilian version = home). You do this so often and with such expertise that it becomes second nature. Your children live and grow knowing and using acronyms that have absolutely no meaning to their civilian peers. Even your pets are part of the system as you move, vaccinate, isolate and quarantine them depending upon where you are coming from and going to.

And then you retire.

In the flash of a moment, certificates are presented, orders are cut, Identification cards are re-done and your entire life status changes. You become a member of another older and not so elite community—that of the "retired" military community. For many soldiers it is a relief, a change long coming and anticipated. For others it is a monumental change to the order of life and a transition full of personal and professional obstacles. For military spouses it is often the end of an era, one that is fraught with emotionally packed challenges. It has often been correlated to dying, without all the ceremonies.

As a military spouse, my personal and professional e-mail boxes used to be filled with information on changes to the regulations, upcoming events, special activities and important news of the day. Some days my incoming messages far outweighed those I sent out. The first change I felt was the day after my Soldier retired and my inboxes showed only thirty new messages; two weeks later, ten new and after a month only three. I thought the rest of the human race had fallen off the planet, but I was wrong—they were still there, it was my world that had changed.

As a military spouse you become privy to conversations and information exchanges about a wide variety of community and military issues and events that affect the lives of soldiers and their families. When you leave that status, for many spouses, you no longer "understand the lifestyle, appreciate the hardships, walk-the-walk" of other family members. You stand in disbelief and awe as you become priority 5 in the pharmacy, hospital and other community agencies. You're taken aback the first time someone points out to (in a not so positive manner) "Oh, you're RETIRED military." (First time someone said this to me I felt like I had contracted leprosy or grown horns and a tail.) Some are envious, some are jealous, others are afraid that they will never reach that point, but all identify with your old role as a military spouse, while you must now adjust to your new one.

There are those who run for the door, arms open wide, embracing the freedom of the civilian world before the ink is dry on the DD 214. These are usually the folks who had a tracking calendar mounted on the wall of every kitchen they occupied, marking off the time until retirement (many began this ritual from the day their Soldier enlisted or they married into the military). They publicly praise the joys and benefits of leaving the military circle, settling down, not moving again until the front lawn overgrows their homes. They empathize with those still moving every three years, draft up mile-long "to do" lists (oddly enough most include—"travel more—to see family, see the country, or just get out of town") and inherently adapt the phrase ".....when I was a military spouse" and "Oh, been there, done that, got the t-shirt."

As the spouse of a RETIRED military person I will:

- Not set the alarm for 0430.
- Remove the "Army Wife" sticker from my rear window and replace it with a new "US Army Wife—Retired" logo.
- Start writing addresses in my address book in ink, not pencil.
- Buy my new home wisely remembering that my potentially obnoxious neighbors may NOT move out in three years.
- Realize that "permanent duty station" now translates into home.
- Plant a tree or bush or garden and know that I will be there to watch it grow.
- Use concrete, not just dirt, to set a fence post (knowing I won't have to tear it up again—ever).
- Learn how to speak to my family and friends using full words, not acronyms.
- Continue to watch the news, just not 24/7— sorry—I mean all day, every day...
- Not growl as he/she complains about how much "stuff" I have, while old TA 50 (field gear) still sits in footlockers in my storage shed.
- Stay in touch with old friends, but remember that their lives have not changed, mine has.

- Identify myself by first and last name, not as "Household 7" or the "wife of 1SG somebody."
- Refer the calls I am still getting from my old Family Readiness Group to the new leader.
- Identify alternate shopping sites in my community that are not the BX, PX, NEX (you get the idea).
- Understand that I can finally throw away all those empty boxes in my barn that I saved to repack my figurines, stereo and computer stuff in (we really do save those for reshipping/ packing needs).

WHEN CHILDREN
BECOME SOLDIERS

One of the most difficult transitions imaginable is that of becoming the mom of a Soldier. I always knew that there was risk in any time that my husband spent deployed away from home. I accepted the constant changes to lifestyle and living conditions. But to accept those same risks for my children was almost impossible.

Deployments, for any Soldier, are a routine and expected part of life and a military spouse knows and accepts this as part of his/her life when they marry into the military. We stand and salute, wave banners and say good-byes, hoping for the best, bracing for the worst. We return to our homes, children in tow, and resume the waiting game once again.

We shield our children from the conflict as much as possible. We set up family times and schedules to share letters and special events either by e-mail or videotape or even web cam with our soldiers so far away. We comfort them as they cry in the night, missing their deployed parent, attend mother/ father or son/daughter events as the missing parent, identify with their desire to have that parent home, and explain that just because the neighbor kid's mom or dad comes home every night and their doesn't, it doesn't make them different from other kids.

And then one morning we wake up and there are two sets of Army uniforms hanging in two different closets. Different sizes of boots stand in silent salute by the front door, one nicked and scratched from daily use and age, the other brilliantly polished, unmarred by wear, field exposure or time. The second pair of boots belongs not just to the Soldier we married, but also to the soldiers to whom we gave birth. The very children that we carried to and through so many years of military exposure have gone and done the unbelievable, but not unpredictable—they have enlisted—and the term deployment takes on a new meaning for most mothers and fathers.

Our children (military brat if you will), raised on MREs, fluent in "militarese" and well-versed on military traditions, grow into sons and daughters. Embroiled in family tradition, home-grown in military culture, they often gravitate to the military commitment for a wide variety of reasons. Family tradition, social expectations, need for college funds or just a simple sense of duty, they raise their right hand and cease to be the "soldier's family," and become the Soldier. It is here that life gets even tougher for the military spouse, now the mom or dad of a Soldier.

We spent a lifetime protecting our children, watching their every move, healing their boo-boos as they happened, soothing crushed hearts, broken dreams, bad skin and a variety of other "crisis issues" that affect the average child growing up. But ours are not the "average child." Routinely they are born in a military hospital, attend military (DoDDS) schools and live on military installations. From birth they are thrown into a culture of service, immersed into a life of Battle Dress Uniforms (BDUs), duffel bags, and then we wonder why they choose to enter a military life also.

I remember, standing in by the kitchen sink in absolute disbelief, as my son—who only the year before had raged through the house cursing the military life and blaming all world crises and situations on the Army—brandished his enlistment papers proudly. His face and eyes glowed more brightly than when he came off the football field after a winning game. "What happened to you? I thought you would have joined a monastery before you would have enlisted?"

He smiled, hugged me and said, quietly and simply, "It's time to give something back." I was never so proud or scared in my entire military life.

EPILOGUE

I have written of my battles and the battles of others that have endured our way of life these many years, not properly recognizing the battles that our Soldiers fight as well. They too endure the hardship of separation, loneliness and fear of loss. We are all Warriors in our own right and continue to fight for those who come after us.

When I began writing *Once in a WifeTime* it was a tribute to the struggles of the military spouse. It has been an evolutionary process and labor of love taking more than 10 years to complete.

Looking back over the 26 years, realizing how my Soldier and I have grown stronger whether together or apart, I am truly blessed to have been able to experience all that I have. As I reviewed the pages of the text, I realized that in all my writings I had not taken the time to tell the one person who made it all possible just how grateful I was to him for all that he gave me. Courage, honor, loyalty, integrity are not just words, but a way of life for my Soldier, my husband, my partner, my soul mate. Without his support, love and devotion, this life, this book would not have been possible. As the result of his many years of exposure to the high intensity of the desert sun, he now wages the greatest battle of his life, the fight against cancer. It may be a battle that he cannot win but as he constantly tells me, "Cancer will know it's been in a real dog fight before I'm done." One dear friend, also a now retired military spouse (don't have many who aren't) cursed the Army life when she learned of my husbands struggle for life. She blamed the Army for taking away all the time in deployments, field exercises, and training trips that could have been better spent with us at home. But the reality is I married a Soldier and the life experiences and exposures that we have shared have given us the strength to face any challenge, overcome any obstacle and adjust to any changes we may have to make to get through this last battle - the battle we fight for us. There are no regrets, no road or path we would change, nothing that we would do any differently than we had done before. My life with my Soldier has truly been a *Once in a WifeTime* journey.